The Spirituality of Money:

Your mistaken beliefs about money could be preventing you from living the life you deserve

The Spirituality of Money:

Your mistaken beliefs about money could be preventing you from living the life you deserve

Mike Morley & Irene McGarvie

Ancient Wisdom Publishing
a division of Nixon-Carre Ltd., Toronto, ON

Library and Archives Canada Cataloguing in Publication

Morley, Michel, 1952-
    The spirituality of money : your mistaken beliefs about money could be preventing you from living the life you deserve / Mike Morley & Irene McGarvie.

Includes index.
ISBN 978-0-9783939-3-9

    1. Finance, Personal--Religious aspects. 2. Money--Religious aspects. 3. Wealth--Religious aspects. I. McGarvie, Irene, 1957- II. Title.
HG179.M675 2009   332.024'01   C2009-901212-X

Published by:
Ancient Wisdom Publishing
A division of Nixon-Carre Ltd.
P.O. Box 92533
Carlton RPO
Toronto, Ontario, M5A 4N9

www.learnancientwisdom.com
www.nixon-carre.com

Distributed by Ingram 1-800-937-8000
www.ingrambook.com

Disclaimer:
This publication is designed to provide accurate and authoritative information. It is sold with the understanding that the publishers are not engaged in rendering legal, medical or other professional advice. If medical or other expert assistance is required, the services of a competent professional should be sought. The information contained herein represents the experiences and opinions of the authors, but the author is not responsible for the results of any action taken on the basis of information in this work, nor for any errors or omissions.

General Notice:
Any product names used in this book are for identification purposes only and may be registered trademarks, or trade names of their respective owners. The authors, Mike Morley and Irene McGarvie, and the publisher, Ancient Wisdom Publishing (a division of Nixon-Carre Ltd.) disclaim any and all rights in those marks.

Printed and bound in the USA

Contents

We can change our experience of the world around us • Watch your words • I only have, I can't afford • Be careful what you wish for • Stop blaming others for your problems • We can control what we think • Delusional thinking • Worry • Like attracts like • Victim or victor • No one can cheat you without your willing participation • You can lead a charmed life

Common myths about money • Traditional Christian beliefs • What is God? • Does God really want us to be poor • Money is the root of all evil • No honest person ever becomes rich • There is only so much money to go around • It is more spiritual to be poor • You must work hard for your money • Money is power • Money does not grow on trees • Save your money if you want to get rich • It takes money to make money • The rich get richer and the poor get poorer • How much money would it take for you to feel comfortable? • God: The universal source of your supply • Prayer

Change is inevitable • Fear of the unknown • The good old days? • What would happen if nothing changed? • Death is inevitable • Fear vs. excitement

Chapter 9 - 8 Steps to real financial security 89

Accept responsibility and release the past • Accept change • See the possibilities • Get definite about what you want • Indulge in "delusional" thinking • Create a vacume to receive • Act as if • Think very carefully before you acquire any new "stuff"

This book is dedicated to the two most
influential women in our lives

Laurette Bourbonnais
&
Jane McGarvie

Business women who were way ahead of their time.

Introduction

There is nothing new in this book. These simple principles have been around for thousands of years.

Traditionally, religions have programmed us to think about money in a way that does not serve our best interests. For example, we may have been taught that wanting money is bad, that too much money is bad, and that people with money are bad. We then feel guilty when we get money, yet money is a necessary part of life. These beliefs keep us constantly confused because we are not sure how to reconcile these two opposing points of view.

The purpose of this book is to help you undo the programming that has kept you from prospering and replace it with principles that have worked for successful people throughout history.

*"All the forms man fashions with his hands
must first exist in thought;
he cannot shape the thing until he has
thought the thing."*

**Wallace Wattles,
The Science of Getting Rich**

Think yourself rich

1

There is only one surefire way to achieve prosperity. It is by altering your thoughts.

> *"All that we are is the result of what*
> *we have thought."*
> **the Buddha**

What a great quote from the Buddha. If we meditate on this concept for a while we soon see that our current financial position is the result of all of our previous thoughts. Whether we are experiencing abundance, or serious financial trouble, we have created it through our thoughts, words, and actions. If we change how we think, talk and act, we will change our lives.

Most people in our society are under the mistaken belief that our lives are shaped by what happens around us and to us, events that are beyond our control. But it is not what happens outside of us, it is what we do or think about what happens that determines our lives. In other words, financial problems are the outer manifestation of our inner state of consciousness. We may have little control of the fluctuation of the stock market or the general state of the economy, but we can control what goes on in our mind.

Changing how we think about money will change how we talk about money (both to others and to ourselves) and will ultimately change how we act regarding money. We can truly think ourselves rich.

We can change our experience of the world around us

Changing how we think changes our expectations. When we change our expectations we prepare for the results we anticipate. Therefore, we are ready for the opportunity when it presents itself. When we respond to the opportunity, it changes how the world in turn responds to us.

For example, if you are expecting to receive employment opportunities (perhaps a job offer or increased sales if you are self employed), then you would ensure that you are ready and available to accommodate the request, and would go out expectantly looking for it, confident that if it didn't happen today then it would happen tomorrow.

However, if you really do not expect to get offered more work you would tend not to prepare to do the work, and not go out expectantly looking for it. Instead, you would say to yourself something to the effect of "What's the point of trying, it isn't going to work anyway." And you would turn on the TV set and sit around feeling sorry for yourself. The world would then cooperate by not beating a path to your door and you would have made your expectation of not being able to earn money come true as a result of your own expectations and attitude.

Watch your words

Notice what happens if you say, *"I have this problem?"* Immediately your mind pictures a difficult situation with impenetrable obstacles. Notice what happens when you replace it with the phrase *"I have this project."* Instantly your mind turns to developing creative solutions.

I only have ... I can't afford ...

When you say or think things like *"I only have"* or *"I can't afford"*, your thoughts are subtly centered on what you do not have, with the subconscious fear that you do not have enough.

How often have you said, *"I can't afford that,"* or *"I couldn't do that."*

Instead, try saying *"What could I do in order to be able to afford that?"* or *"How could I do that?"*

Making a little change like this opens up a world of possibilities. Opportunities present themselves and the universe lines up to make it possible.

Be careful what you wish for

I know a woman who was working at a job she despised. She desperately wanted to quit, but the benefits were too good. Unfortunately, life often has a funny way of accommodating our innermost heartfelt wishes. Within a year she was diagnosed with cancer. She got sick enough to qualify for her employer's excellent disability payments, but was too sick to enjoy life as she had planned, and unfortunately she may not last long enough to benefit from her employer's generous pension plan. This definitely wasn't what she had in mind.

What are some things I have been thinking and saying that are not producing the results I want in my life?

_____

_____

_____

_____

_____

_____

_____

_____

_____

_____

_____

Stop blaming others for your problems

"Always when there seems to be delay, confusion, or a block between you and your good, that block lies within you, and not in some outside circumstance or personality."
Catherine Ponder,
The Secret of Unlimited Prosperity

If we are serious about changing our financial situation the first step is taking personal responsibility for our lives and for our previous choices. This is the most important thing we can do. No more blaming other people or circumstances.

Blaming our present situation on our childhood experiences is futile. We can blame our parents for an unhappy childhood, our teachers for our failure in school, the government for messing up the economy, the union for not protecting us, or the doctor for not being able to find a drug to cure us, but that does not change our present predicament. Taking personal responsibility is the only way things will improve.

Some people argue that saying we are responsible is too simplistic, they point out that a child growing up in poverty has no control of their situation. This is true, but once that child becomes an adult they do have choices and it does not benefit anyone to claim that their bad childhood is holding them back. Many very wealthy people throughout history started off with huge handicaps but managed to succeed, while you see others who seemingly have everything going for them and they fail at everything they do. As adults we have a choice, we can decide to stay in our old patterns, blaming others for our problems, and suffering more of the same, or we can choose to accept responsibility and move on.

Old habits die hard and new ones are very difficult to establish and maintain. Whenever you find yourself thinking or saying something from your past that does not serve you well, ask yourself "Does believing this help me or hinder me?" Is this an old habit trying to reestablish itself?

Who or what have I been blaming for my current financial situation?

_____

_____

_____

_____

_____

_____

_____

_____

_____

We can control what we think

We control what we think, and how we interpret a particular experience or event. No one can force us to think a particular way if we consciously choose not to.

As long as we are consciously aware of what we are thinking we can decide how we feel and determine the effect it will have on our life. For example, if someone seems to be staring at me, I can either decide that they are being rude and thinking that I am fat or ugly, or I can decide that they are looking at me because they think I look nice and they think they know me and are trying to remember my name. If I interpret their behavior the first way it feels threatening but the second way does not. The interpretation I choose determines how I feel and ultimately how I react.

Delusional thinking?

By choosing to think pleasant thoughts am I just deluding myself? Perhaps, but it certainly makes me feel better at the time, and changes how people respond to me. People like to be around people who make them feel good. When you are pleasant, you attract people and opportunities. If you are in a bad mood, people do not want to be with you and you push away the opportunities. The expression "Fake it till you make it" means that if you are unhappy, you can deliberately make yourself happy if you work at presenting a happy face to the world.

Regardless of whether you project happiness or misery, the effect is contagious to those around you.

You can acknowledge the reality of a situation, but not its permanence

If something unpleasant occurs we can view it as a changing experience that is on its way out, knowing that something better is on the way. Don't dwell on the negative. Don't even try to explain why it happened, just let it go. Start again picturing and expecting what you want. We invite good things by dwelling on good things.

Worry

> *"For the thing which I greatly feared is come upon me..."*
> **Job 3:25**

What you focus on grows. It is a universal law that the thoughts that we hold in our mind influence our circumstances. Worry is visualizing some undesirable condition coming about. Therefore, the conditions you worry about will probably happen.

It is a universal law that what you think about, you attract. If you spend your time thinking thoughts of lack and failure, you will attract lack and failure, but if you concentrate your thoughts on abundance, you will attract abundance to you.

Like attracts like

You attract to you people who think the same kind of

thoughts that you do. We see this law in action in the business world. The person who dwells upon thoughts of goodness and success, will radiate goodness and attract customers and success. But the person who dwells on negative thoughts, seeing only the problems and troubles of the world, sets up a negative mental atmosphere that repels customers and success.

In order to experience abundance, the first thing you need to overcome is the feeling of needing money. Most people with problems tend to concentrate on them, and then wonder why they continue to have them. What is the first thing that people think and say during periods of financial adversity? "I need money!" But what you really need is faith, and a flow of creativity. You need ideas!

Any idea exclusively occupying the mind turns into reality.

We become what we think about most of the time

> *"Every day and in every way I am getting better and better."*
> **Émile Coué**

Émile Coué (1857-1926) was a French pharmacist and psychologist who discovered "the placebo effect". He observed that a person's mental state is able to influence the effect of medications. As a psychologist at The Lorraine Society of Applied Psychology he developed a method of self-improvement that he called optimistic autosuggestion. He observed that his patients could cure themselves more efficiently by replacing their "thought of illness" with a new "thought of cure". In other words, repeating words or images enough times causes the subconscious mind to absorb them.

So, what are you thinking about most of the time, thoughts of abundance or thoughts of lack? The results of what you are thinking will show up all around you.

Victim or victor

When it comes to financial issues, whether you feel that you can control what happens to you or that you are only a victim of circumstances is up to you. When you decide to be in control, you can do something constructive and change how you react. It really is all in your mind.

Think of a situation in your life where you could choose a different explanation for why something has happened.

_____

_____

_____

_____

_____

No one can cheat you without your willing participation

If you feel you have been cheated by a business partner or in your divorce, it is easy to blame your misfortune on the other person when if fact you have contributed to the situation. Even if you are not initially totally convinced that you caused it, just begin to entertain the idea and if you are totally honest with yourself you will soon begin to see ways in which you contributed to the situation. No one can cheat you without your willing participation.

I once had a couple of friends who were business partners. When the business failed, I asked each one separately what happened. The first one complained how the other had sabotaged everything by not communicating when things started going downhill. When I asked the other partner, I got the same story in reverse. After each had calmed down a little, they both admitted that they were to blame to some extent because they should have taken the initiative and worked things out. It's too bad they could not have figured that out before the business failed and each had lost a serious amount of money.

As I write the update to this book, Bernie Madoff has been sentenced to 150 years in jail for swindling people out of at least $50 billion of their life savings. The interesting thing is that most people suspected that his returns were too good to be true. Many people knew that he was perpetrating a fraud, but turned a blind eye because they thought they were sharing in the money he was making. The majority of his victims effectively "allowed" themselves to be taken because they chose to ignore the warning signs of fraud.

Have you ever felt that you were cheated by someone?
In what way did you contribute to what happened?

_____

_____

_____

_____

_____

_____

_____

_____

_____

Accepting personal responsibility is a characteristic of successful people. Understanding that you attract into your life all the experiences, both good and bad, through your thoughts is the most important step in thinking yourself rich.

You can lead a charmed life

When you are in charge of your mind, and work with the creative flow, instead of against it, everything seems to go your way: parking spaces open up for you; business opportunities seem to fall out of the sky; people are fair in their dealings with you; jobs appear; promotions come. Your prosperity is not dependent on luck or by changes in the economy. You can control your luck.

"You must get rid of the last vestige of the old idea that there is a deity whose will it is that you should be poor, or whose purposes may be served by keeping you in poverty."

**Wallace Wattles,
The Science of Getting Rich**

Change the way you think about God

2

Common myths about money - by Irene

We have all grown up with certain notions about money. These notions vary greatly depending on our culture, religious background, and social upbringing. Unfortunately, many of our notions about money and spirituality do not serve us well.

Traditional Christian beliefs

Traditional Christian teachings have sometimes misinterpreted Christ's teachings about prosperity. Mike's Catholic upbringing included what he calls the "martyrdom" factor which honors suffering and poverty as a way of earning your way to heaven.

Some people believe in destiny. In other words, where you end up is preordained by God and there is nothing you can do about it. You should be content with your lot.

What is God?

Is there an "intelligent design" that organizes the universe? Agnostics and atheists would argue that God is just a "concept"; something that people pretend exists in order to fill a psychological need.

Who or what is God to you? Is God an old guy with a beard sitting on a cloud that keeps track of what you do - an accountant continually tallying up debits and credits, a benevolent dictator who decides our fate and punishes us when we are "bad?"

As a Spiritualist minister the concept of God as a benevolent dictator does not work for me. I prefer the monistic theory of the universe which is the theory that one is all, and that all is one; in other words, we are all connected, and one substance makes up the seemingly many elements of the material world. This theory is the foundation of all the Oriental philosophies and has been gradually winning its way into Western thought for the past 200 years.

I think of God as the natural energy/power of the universe, an energy that we all can access, and is in all of us. In other words, God is a participative democracy to which each of us belongs. This implies that each of us is part of God and we as individuals must do our part. Accepting this sort of personal responsibility can be terrifying at first, but exhilarating once you begin to see the possibilities.

So, who or what is God to you? Has your concept of God empowered you, or held you back up to now?

_____

_____

_____

_____

_____

_____

_____

_____

_____

Does God really want us to be poor?

The only benefit to being poor accrues to the organized church and politicians. Keeping the faithful and the population in a constant state of want and fear of losing what they have keeps them obedient. The news media are collaborators in perpetuating this state of fear. Even the weather channels contribute by imploring viewers to stay tuned for the latest on the bad weather coming which helps them sell commercials. But this strategy no longer works once people realize that it is they who have the real power, not the leaders to whom they have abdicated responsibility for their lives in the past.

10 of the most common misconceptions about God and money that have been holding us back

Misconception #1: Money is the root of all evil

This is one of the most misquoted of all Bible verses. The actual quote is:

"The love of money is the root of all evil."
1 Timothy 6:10

Money itself is neither good nor evil. What counts is your attitude towards money.

Having money is not an end in itself. Money is simply a means of achieving your other goals in life. Money is just energy that can be exchanged for other energy. The exchange between two willing parties must be mutually beneficial. In fact, each must receive more value than what they have paid for. This is how the constant exchange of money builds wealth. When the exchanges stop, financial growth is stifled. This is what we have experienced during this recent economic "downturn." People are afraid to spend money freely so the exchange of money slows down and everyone suffers.

What do you believe about money?

_____

_____

_____

Misconception #2: No honest person ever becomes rich

"For it is easier for a camel to go through a needle's eye, than for a rich man to enter into the kingdom of God."
Luke 18:25 KJV, also Matthew 19:24, Mark 10:25.

Is this verse referring to attempting to push a camel through the eye of a sewing needle? If so, it would certainly seem to convey the idea that it is impossible for a rich person to get into heaven.

However, if you understand that the Eye of the Needle was a doorway in Jerusalem where camels had to be unloaded and drop their heads in order to access the city, it takes on an entirely different meaning.

Yes, it is true that some dishonest people have lots of money. However, unless they change their beliefs about money, the money will not make them very happy. I think that what this verse is actually saying is that your attitudes about money can be more of a burden than a blessing for some people. Honest people with the right attitude towards money can have money and the feelings of comfort and security that comes with it.

Misconception #3: There is only so much money to go around

The concept of scarcity and competition is such a pervasive myth that we have devoted an entire chapter to it, but for now, believe it when we say that there is plenty of money to go around. Money and wealth are continually being created. If money is continually flowing the supply is endless. Getting the money you want will not reduce the available supply for others so there is no need to feel guilty about success. Shortages only occur when individuals attempt to hoard money and things in an unsuccessful attempt to feel secure.

In **2 Kings 4:1-7** we read the story about the prophet Elisha and the poor widow who is being hounded by her creditors. When she tells him that all she has in the house is a little oil Elisha tells the widow to go to her neighbors and borrow as many jars as she can. He begins to pour the oil from her container into the borrowed containers and when all the borrowed jars were filled the oil stopped.

This story suggests the need to expand our minds to include new possibilities. In other words, as much as we can conceive and believe, we can receive.

Do you believe that money is scarce? If so, that will be your experience. I find it much more effective to believe that there is a never ending supply, I just need to bring on the jars and they will be filled.

Misconception #4: It is more spiritual to be poor. God loves poor people more than rich people.

"And he lifted up his eyes on his disciples, and said, Blessed be ye poor: for yours is the kingdom of God."
Luke 6:20 (KJV)

"Blessed are the poor in spirit: for theirs

is the kingdom of heaven."
Matthew 5:3 (KJV)

Hmmm, these verses certainly make it seem like poor people get to go to heaven, but what about the following verses:

"Certain women…. ministered unto him of their substance"
Luke 8:2-3 (KJV)

Apparently Jesus and his disciples weren't just living on nothing. It is pretty obvious that some of His followers were women with money who paid much of the expenses. It is difficult to be generous and support worthy causes when you are broke.

In Matthew 17:24-27 Jesus and his disciples have to come up with some money to pay a tax assessment. So Jesus tells Peter, the fisherman, to go and catch a fish, and in the mouth of which he would find a gold coin. Was this a miracle as some people assume? No, there are no miracles in an orderly universe. What Jesus was saying to Peter was there is money in fish, in other words, go out and bring in a catch of fish, sell it in the marketplace, and we will have enough money to pay the tax.

"The Kingdom of God is within you."
Luke 17:21 (KJV)

What Jesus is saying here is that within every person there is limitless access to infinite intelligence. What this means is that we already have access to everything that we need in order to be happy, healthy and wealthy. Anything that we appear to lack is the result of some sort of blockage in the free flow of the creative process, something that we have done to ourselves. In other words, poverty is the result of a blockage in the creative process.

Misconception #5: You must work hard for your money

"In the sweat of thy face shalt thou eat bread, till thou return unto the ground..."
Genesis 3:19

This is where God curses Adam for disobeying his order not to eat from the tree in the center of the Garden of Eden. The curse seems to be that man will have to toil hard for his food until the day he dies.

However, there is another possible explanation. Instead of being a curse directed against Adam for transgressing one of God's arbitrary rules, this story symbolizes the breaking of natural law: if you attempt to break any of the natural laws you will have to struggle and work a lot harder than is necessary. In this case, Adam was going to have to plant his own crops (instead of eating what God had already planted) and work a lot harder than he had been previously. What this means for us is that if we work with the natural laws of the universe, instead of trying to go against them, things will be easier for us.

If you are working at the right job for you, doing something that utilizes your unique gifts, it won't feel like drudgery, more like play, and you will be amazed that you are actually being paid for doing something that you would probably be willing to do for free.

The belief that it takes a lifetime to get rich is an extension of the myth that you must work hard for your money. New billionaires who get rich almost overnight do it through creative ideas, not by slaving away their entire lives. Sacrificing fifty years or so of your working life to save for a short retirement that may never arrive is absurd. There must be a balance between preparing for the future and "enjoying the now." In life there are no guarantees, only possibilities.

If you need proof that it doesn't have to take a lifetime to amass a fortune look at these self-made millionaire teenagers:

Internet millionaire Cameron Johnson

Cameron began his first business at the age of 9 making and selling greeting cards. By the time he was 15 years old, he was earning $300,000 to $400,000 a month, and by age 19, he had sold just one of his numerous Web sites for more than a million dollars.

Internet millionaire siblings Catherine & Dave Cook

Catherine, aged 15, and her brother Dave, aged 17, came up with the idea to develop a free online version of their high school yearbook. Within one year MyYearbook had raised $4.1 million of venture capital. The business has grown to 3 million members worldwide; and earns annual advertising sales in the "seven figures."

Home-made jam tycoon Fraser Doherty

At the age of 14, Doherty started making jam in the kitchen of his parents home in Scotland. Six years later, SuperJam is now on the shelves of most U.K. supermarkets, with annual sales of more than £1.5 million. Fraser's net worth is now estimated at approximately £2 million, which proves that you don't have to be a high tech wizard to make a fortune.

Misconception #6: Money is power

While it is true that having money can give you a certain amount of power to influence people and situations, the real power lies in your mind and in your beliefs about money, and what you do with your money.

The story of Oskar Schindler is a particularly inspirational example of someone who used his money/power to help others during a particularly reprehensible time in our history.

Schindler is credited with saving almost 1,200 Jews from death during the Holocaust by employing them in his factories in Poland and the Czech Republic. His story is told in the book Schindler's Ark, and the film based on it, Schindler's List.

Oskar Schindler was a member of the Nazi party, a businessman initially motivated by money (Jewish forced labor was cheap), but after witnessing a 1943 raid on the Kraków ghetto, he was appalled by the murder of Jews and began shielding his workers without regard for the cost.

He would claim that unskilled workers, wives, children, and even handicapped persons were necessary mechanics and metalworkers essential to the war effort. He typically bribed government officials to look the other way.

In one of his factories, which produced missiles and hand grenades for the war effort, not a single weapon produced could actually be fired.

He also began smuggling children out of the Jewish ghetto, delivering them to Polish nuns, who either hid them from the Nazis or claimed they were Christian orphans.

By the end of the war Schindler was broke, his money having been spent bribing officials and caring for his workers.

So, what could the power of money do for you?

_____

_____

_____

_____

_____

_____

_____

_____

_____

Misconception #7: Money does not grow on trees

This was one of my father's favorite expressions. That and *"Who do you think I am Rockefeller?"* What these expressions convey is the belief that money is hard to come by.

"Who do you think you are, Andrew Carnegie?" was his way of saying that we should lower our expectations. For my father, growing up in extreme poverty, that was his reality, but, my reality is that there is no need to lower my expectations. There's plenty to go around. While money may not grow on trees (unless you own an orchard?) it can be virtually plucked out of the air in the form of creative ideas.

Samuel Clemens' (Mark Twain) first publishing business failed. He lost everything and he was forced into bankruptcy. He then embarked on a successful speaking tour in order to pay off his creditors even though he was under no legal obligation to do so and soon rebuilt his fortune. He is a true example of someone who plucked his fortune out of the air in the form of creative ideas.

Misconception #8: Save your money if you want to get rich

"A penny saved is a penny earned."

In my Scottish family the importance of thrift was always emphasized. While I still recognize the value of frugality, as I become more familiar with natural law, I have come to realize that too much emphasis on saving and budgeting causes you to focus on lack, which actually blocks the flow of energy and keeps you poor.

> *"There is that scattereth, and yet increaseth; and there is that withholdeth more than is meet, but it tendeth to poverty. The liberal soul shall be made fat: and he that watereth shall be watered also himself."*
> **Proverbs 11:24, 25 (KJV)**

Giving and spending freely is an important part of feeling abundant. This verse from Proverbs describes the seeming contradiction that the generous person increases his net worth while the person that hoards stays poor. You see it with some people who lived through very difficult times. They have such a fear of lack that they hoard everything they can get their hands on, afraid to part with anything, until their homes become so clogged with "stuff" that there is no room to move. The premise behind the practice of Feng Shui is that energy needs to move, and hoarding of belongings, which is an attempt to feel secure, blocks the flow of energy.

An addiction to constantly accumulating goods is a result of the fear of not having enough combined with the belief that there is a limited supply. Both wealth and poverty are a frame of mind rather than a financial state. Your thoughts, expectations, and actions determine your fate.

We must give freely if we are to receive freely. No matter what our current situation is, we always have something to give. When you think you can't afford to give is exactly the time when you cannot afford not to give.

"Give, and it shall be given unto you; good measure, pressed down, and shaken together, and running over, shall men give into your bosom. For with the same measure that ye mete withal it shall be measured to you again."
Luke 6:38

We have seen this principle in action many times. Once when our financial resources were very shaky we decided to put it to the test. A friend was having an art show and we decided to purchase one of her paintings in order to encourage her in her career. Buying a painting would seem to be a very foolish thing to do given our circumstances at the time, but we decided to step out in faith. The very next day Mike was engaged to do a large consulting project that returned the money tenfold.

"Getting rich is not the result of saving, or thrift; many very penurious people are poor, while free spenders often get rich."
Wallace Wattles,
The Science of Getting Rich

Misconception #9: It takes money to make money

This is an excuse for accepting things as they are. I can't make money because I don't have any seed capital. It is easier to believe this myth than to acknowledge that you already have access to everything that you need.

There are plenty of people in the world with money who are desperate to place their money in good investments. Ideas are much more valuable than money. If you have a good enough idea the money will pour in. If the universe can give you the idea it can most certainly provide the money.

Once you recognize that making and having money depends on how you think, talk, and act, then you will soon see that starting off with money is not a prerequisite.

Misconception #10: The rich get richer, the poor get poorer

"For unto every one that hath shall be given, and he shall have abundance: but from him that hath not shall be taken away even that which he hath."
Matthew 25:29 KJV

At first glance this verse seems to say that the rich get richer and the poor get poorer, which doesn't seem fair. But what Jesus is doing in this verse is explaining one of the natural laws of the universe which is that we get more of what we expect, in this case the rich expect to be rich while the poor fear losing the little they have.

I had a university professor who was a Marxist-Lennonist and one of his favorite expressions was "You stay where you start", meaning that people remain close to the socio-economic status into which they were born. This certainly tends to be true, but not because there is some kind of plot on the part of the rich to keep the poor down, but because we are influenced by the people we associate with. When you are born into money, you see different possibilities than those who are born into poverty.

Farrah Gray in his excellent book *"Get Real, Get Rich"* describes how for people living in poverty it is as if they were surrounded by a wall of mirrors. They only know what they see. They only see the poverty and the limitations reflected back to them. This is reality to them. To get out of the trap they are in they somehow need to be able to jump up and peek over the wall to see all the possibilities beyond.

Traveling and seeing places and people outside your immediate world shows you there is not only one reality, but many other possible realities. Everyone has more options than they think. You really can go from rags to riches through the power of your thoughts.

How much money would it take for you to feel comfortable?

If you ask people this question you will invariably find that the amount of money that they claim they would need to have in order to feel comfortable is a number a little bit more than what they currently have. It doesn't matter if they currently earn $20,000 a year, or $20 million. Once you reach that higher number you soon find that even that much isn't quite enough. Enough is elusive.

God: The universal source of your supply

If you are depending on money to give you security it will never happen. The only real security is your belief that the universe is a kind loving place, that everything works together for your good, and that your belief that things will work out will see you through.

If you believe that God is in all of us and we are all part of God, that we are inter-dependent and that we are each other's supply of wealth, then there is no need to worry that our only source will dry up. The number of sources and ways of having money come to you are limitless. You just need to get rid of your misconceptions about how these sources will provide you with money. There are money making opportunities around us all of the time, but most of us do not see them when they are presented to us because we do not expect to see them.

Prayer

"Fear not, little flock; for it is your Father's good pleasure to give you the kingdom."
Luke 12:32 (KJV)

This verse certainly seems to indicate that God wants to give us what we want, so why is it that we pray as though we were supplicating a capricious God? Please, please, please!

We behave like toddlers in the cereal aisle at the grocery store, nagging at God until we get what we want. Gimme, gimme, gimme! But until we understand that God is not a super person to whom we pray and from whom we beg favors, unless we begin to understand the concept of God as principle, you will go on living a marginal existence.

> *"For your Father knoweth what things ye*
> *have need of, before ye ask him."*
> **Matthew 6:8 (KJV)**

If God knows what we need, then why do we have to pray for it? We have been conditioned to think of prayer as a magic catalyst that makes God work for us. Prayer does not make God work nor does it release some kind of miracle power. There are no miracles in an orderly universe. The primary reason for praying is to get a clear picture in our mind of what we want. We are creating the condition in our mind that makes the result inevitable. All we need is to know what we want, and want it badly enough so that it will stay in our thoughts. Through prayer we are in effect claiming what is already ours.

> *"If a person would have his prayers answered he must be*
> *willing to be a channel through which the prayers of others*
> *are answered. If he would be healed he must be willing to*
> *be a healer of discords. If he would have prosperity he must*
> *be willing to become still and face the issue honestly."*
> **Francis W. Foulks,**
>
> **Effectual Prayer**

3

Change how you think about change

Change is inevitable - by Mike

Growth and change are the one constant in life. You are either growing or you are dying. In my years in the corporate world, I have seen people who try to coast in their jobs till retirement time only to be startled to find themselves out of a job. There is no sitting still; you are either moving with the current or you are about to get knocked over.

It's like the whitewater canoeing course Irene and I took. We were taught that if we capsized we needed to keep our feet up and flow with the current so we wouldn't get caught in the rocks and drown. We had to be able to keep moving or we would drown. In life, you can't let your feet get caught under the rocks; you have to keep moving with the flow of change.

There is a plaque on a bridge over the Don River in Toronto that says:

"This river I step in is not the river I stand in."

In other words, the river is always flowing and the water where you are never stays the same.

Most of the stress in our lives is created by trying to control circumstances that are outside of our control. Trying to prevent change is like trying to stop your car by dragging your feet, it doesn't work and it hurts.

Fear of the unknown

People do not like change because they fear the unknown. Change is scary. It means all your plans have to change just when you thought you had it all figured out. Just when you thought you had it made, the things you thought would see you through are disappearing.

How you choose to think about change will determine whether change is a good or a bad thing for you. If you decide that change is both inevitable and good you will accept it and adjust to it positively. If you decide that change is bad you will fight it, and be run over in the process. Accepting the need for change and recognizing that it is beneficial for everyone in the long run is the key to lifelong happiness.

Most people expect that the "wise" financial decisions of the past will continue to work for them into the future; but the assumptions people made in the past may no longer be valid in the future. Demographics are constantly changing our investment decisions. Baby boomers that have become "empty nesters" are now downsizing and making big houses a liability and health care costs are increasing due to the same aging boomers. They are inheriting the assets their parents accumulated, creating the greatest generational transfer of wealth in history. The cost of fuel is affecting urban planning decisions and is triggering the revitalization of many of our downtown areas. Whether you consider these changes "good" or "bad" depends on how you look at it.

The good old days?

Nothing is more constant than change itself. When my father was a young man in the 1950's, the average price for modest single family home was around $11,000 and $85 a week was a very good pay. Cars cost about $750, bread was 10 cents a loaf, and bus fare was 5 cents. A family could live on one income.

It sounds idyllic, but it also had its problems. Polio was still a deadly disease in the 1950's, fear of nuclear war hung over everyone's heads, and working conditions were not as safe as they are today. Nobody who thinks it through completely would really want to go back to that point in time.

People who grew up during the Great Depression of the 1930's knew what being hungry and having no prospect for a job felt like. It paralyzed some people, and caused them to live in fear for the rest of their lives, yet other individuals saw the opportunities and made their fortunes during these "tough" times.

Everything runs in cycles, so even the Great Depression

of the 1930's could not last forever. The post-war boom times that followed in the 40's, 50's, and 60's was followed by inflation in the seventies and a recession in the eighties. We enjoyed the high tech boom of the 90's which led to the current economic downturn. But remember, even this current situation will not last.

Currently, the US auto industry is going through a disastrous change or a necessary but overdue rebirth, depending on your point of view. For the workers who depend on their union job and company pensions to provide them with financial security, there is at first an angry realization that the promises they were given will be broken. For consumers, the cars they have come to know and love may not be made any more. Everyone will be affected, but it was inevitable. The US auto industry's has been losing its competitive advantage for many years to other car makers. The Big Three need to reinvent themselves to meet the changing times if they hope to be successful again. Workers and retirees will have to do the same. They will need to develop other strategies to compensate for what they think they have lost.

What we are seeing in the auto industry is nothing new. Industries come and go regularly. For example, the automobile industry put buggy whip manufacturers out of business; the cotton gin transformed the economy of the US in 1794 and had a huge impact on the institution of slavery in the Southern United States. Eddy Match Company, one of my previous employers, flourished for nearly 60 years and then disappeared due to the invention of the disposable lighter and the recognition of the health hazards of smoking.

Competitive advantage is something a company has

when it has a jump on its competitors in some way, such as being the first in with a new product, or having the only cheap supply of product, or a monopoly position in the market. However, over time, a company's competitive advantage always disappears because competitors come out with a similar or better product, or can offer a better price, or the company is no longer a monopoly. This is the same for all companies. They have to continually be creating the next competitive advantage because the one they are enjoying now will not last. People have to act accordingly. If their employer is not working on the next big idea, the next competitive advantage, perhaps it is time to find one that is.

Jobs follow companies that have a competitive advantage, even if they are outside the country. We have seen the move from agricultural jobs to manufacturing jobs in the 20th century. Manufacturing jobs always move to where the cost of labor is lowest because low labor costs provide a competitive advantage to companies. As labor rates rise, the company becomes less competitive and the jobs move to countries with a lower cost of labor. This is a constant cycle. The North American manufacturing industry has proven this to be true. North American manufacturers cannot sell products at prices that cover the high costs of producing them in the U.S. and Canada. They have lost their competitive advantage to foreign companies with lower labor costs.

Successful people are constantly reinventing themselves. Successful people anticipate change and are constantly preparing for it. They are always busy preparing financially and getting the education they will need in the future. Their attitude is positive and so they are able to take advantage of the opportunities that arise.

Previous generations could work in a factory for 30-40 years and retire with a good pension and benefits, but that is no longer the reality. The increasing rate of change means that we will be re-inventing ourselves many times over our lifetime.

The ocean is constantly moving and changing. It is a force that we are powerless to control. We delude ourselves into thinking that we have the forces of nature under our control and then events like the sinking of the Titanic, Hurricane Katrina, or the Tsunami of 2006 come along and remind us just how powerless we are. We have to learn to work with the forces of the universe just like we work with the forces of nature, and float along with the change that is inevitable.

What would happen if nothing changed?

If change stopped, life as we know it would stop. For example if the Earth stopped turning, the ocean and wind would stop moving, day and night would stop, creating catastrophic changes in the weather. Daytime would get unendurably hot, and nightime unbearably cold. The world needs to keep moving in order for us to stay alive.

Death is inevitable

Death is also inevitable. We delude ourselves by thinking that if we eat right and exercise we can live forever. My peer group of aging baby boomers are desperately trying to stay young through face lifts and other cosmetic surgery, but the passage of time is becoming obvious judging by the growing number of hips and knees that are having to be replaced. Advances in medicine delude us into thinking that everything can be healed if we can just find the right treatment, the right drug.

The desire for immortality has prompted some to freeze their bodies in the hopes of being revived sometime in the future. But what they don't realize is that these human bodies of ours are only shells that temporarily house the immortal being inside.

If the human race ever managed to become immortal or extend our lifetimes significantly, there would be substantial overpopulation. The resulting stretching of available resources would inevitably lead to conflict and wars over food and land.

We don't really want to stop change, what we want is for things to change our way!

Fear vs. excitement

Some people enjoy the adrenaline rush that comes with fear and interpret it as excitement they are willing to pay for. This explains the popularity of roller coasters, horror films, and extreme sports. Whether the same physiological sensation is interpreted as fear or excitement depends on how they think about it.

The same change in point of view can be used to re-interpret problems as opportunities. For example, an employee can choose to consider a layoff as an opportunity to try a whole new career by reinventing themselves rather than viewing it as a problem they cannot resolve. Even an unexpected, unwanted divorce can be seen as an opportunity to experience a new life with new people.

I heard the Dalai Lama describe our time on earth as tourism. We come here for a short period of time to see new things and have an adventure. Some people come for a short visit, others come for an extended trip. Regardless of how long you have do you really want to spend your time here at the same resort, doing the same things, over and over again?

Change is good.

What changes am I afraid of?

_____

_____

_____

_____

_____

_____

_____

_____

_____

What opportunities are in front of me at the moment?

_____

_____

_____

_____

_____

_____

_____

_____

_____

_____

_____

_____

_____

"You are here on earth to create, not to compete for what it is already created. You do not have to take anything away from anyone. You do not have to drive sharp bargains. You do not need to let any man work for you for less than he earns. You do not have to covet the property of others, or to look at it with wishful eyes; no man has anything of which you cannot have the like, and that without taking what he has away from him. You are to become a creator, not a competitor; you are going to get what you want, but in such a way that when you get it every other man will have more than he has now."

**Wallace Wattles,
The Science of Getting Rich**

4

Change how you think about competition

Creativity vs. Competition - by Irene

When it comes to their job or their business, most people are worried about the competition. They are worried that someone is after their job or after their customers. This is a common fear. It stems from the belief that the supply of money, jobs, and customers is limited. If the supply is limited, you have to fight for your share.

Do you believe it is a "zero sum game" where you need to wrestle your competition for the prize? If yes, you will always be looking over your shoulder, fearing that you will lose your hard-won money, job, or customers to the competition. Riches realized on the competitive plane are never permanent; they are yours today, and someone else's tomorrow.

Once you really understand that your source of money, of employment, or of customers is limitless, that fear goes away. How do you access this limitless supply? You must get rid of all thought of competition. You access the limitless supply by switching from a "competitive" mode to a "creative" mode.

Creativity is necessary for the real creation of wealth. If you are creating something that is unique to you, valuable to others, and lets you be you, you will create sustainable wealth.

I remember seeing a video where the employees in a fish store decided to be creative in serving customers and made singing and having fun part of the shopping experience. The business went from being almost bankrupt to having people line up for the experience of buying fish there. They stopped worrying about the competition and concentrated on new ways of entertaining their customers. As long as they remained in "creative" mode, competition was not a problem.

The business cycle

Just like waves on the beach, there is a natural ebb and flow in business. Initially someone comes up with an idea for a new product or service. Because for a while they are the only one out there they have the "competitive advantage" and they reap the benefits.

Over time imitators come in and start to service the potential customers that the original business wasn't able to service. This is still a good time, everyone is still making money.

But then, over time, competitors move in and try to take a piece of the business for themselves by under-pricing the original. These competitors fight amongst each other for the scraps of business, lowering prices, and lowering quality, until no one is making any money and the business dies out. This is a very bad time for businesses operating on the competitive plane.

Meanwhile the creative business person has already moved on to their next creative idea, in effect plucking money out of thin air.

The creative person never has to worry about competition

You don't have to be an imitator, and you certainly don't have to be a competitor. You never have to fight for scraps. You never have to worry that you will lose what you want because someone else "beats you to it." That cannot possibly happen; you are not seeking anything that belongs to anyone else, you are creating your own, and the supply is limitless. Ideas will come to you as fast as you can receive and use them.

The universe will give you what you want, but it will not take things away from someone else and give them to you. You do not have to be envious of what someone else has, because you can have something equally good.

Many people are under the mistaken notion that the business world is "dog eat dog." There will always be people who think that you need to struggle and fight, but you do not have to play the game that way.

Selling icebergs to Eskimos

I'm sure you have heard the expression, "He could sell icebergs to Eskimos." Referring to a person who could convince someone to buy something that they don't need.

But you don't have to cheat people. You don't have to strike tough bargains in order to make money. You don't have to sell someone something that they don't need.

Those kinds of business practices might seem to work in the short term, but to be successful over the long term you must give your customers more value than the cash value that they give you. Long-term sales success is all about relationships. If you cheat someone once you can be sure that they will not buy from you again.

This works as much for employees as for business owners. Are you giving your employer more value than he pays you for? If not, how long do you think you will have a job?

When you give people more than you take from them you are benefiting everyone through your every business transaction.

Dissatisfaction is a great motivator

Great ideas often spring from a sense of dissatisfaction with the way things currently are. Laziness is not necessarily a bad thing if it results in some creative ideas for change. I'm sure the person who came up with the idea of farming rather than hunting/gathering was probably just tired of continually moving around and wanted to put down roots in a pleasant spot.

Ideas make all the difference

Look at the following ideas and imagine what our world would be like without them:

Paper	The wheel
Eyeglasses	Electricity
The toilet	Sewing machines

Your multi-million dollar idea is right in front of you

Being bad at something could be your ticket to fortune. That is exactly what happened in the case of Bette Nesmith Graham.

In 1951 she was a divorcee who needed to find a job to support herself and her son. She found office work, but she wasn't a very good typist so she came up with the idea of using white tempura paint to cover up her mistakes. In her kitchen at home she developed a product that she called "Mistake Out" and other office workers began to buy it from her. She tried to sell "Mistake Out" to IBM but they turned it down (big mistake on their part) so she changed the name to "Liquid Paper" and continued selling it herself. In 1979 the Gillette Corporation bought Liquid Paper for $47.5 million.

A little trivia tidbit for all you baby boomers: Bette Nesmith Graham was also the mother of Michael Nesmith of "The Monkees."

Analyze your business transactions very carefully. Are you a creator, or an imitator, or a competitor?

"Every man who becomes rich by competition throws down behind him the ladder by which he rises, and keeps others down; but every man who gets rich by creation opens a way for thousands to follow him, it inspires them to do so."

Wallace Wattles,
The Science of Getting Rich

Change how you think about "stuff" 5

The late comedian George Carlin did a famous skit about "stuff." In it he said that a house is "a pile of stuff with a cover on it." He commented that when we travel we have to bring our "stuff" with us so that we feel "at home." He was very funny because he was describing exactly what most of us do. We tend to identify with the things we accumulate. The more we accumulate, the more our ego is flattered.

You can never accumulate enough "stuff" to make you feel secure

In the "Sermon on the Mount", Jesus said:

"Do not lay up for yourselves treasures on earth, where moth and rust consume and where thieves break in and steal, but lay up for yourselves treasures in heaven, where neither moth nor rust consumes and where thieves do not break in and steal. For where your treasure is, there will your heart be also."
Matthew 6:19-21

Jesus was talking about what we think about and how we feel, not just how we act. He was saying that we need to be aware of how we view our "stuff." He warned that people who think their security comes from "stuff" will be continually worried and unhappy.

A person who understands that God/the universe (which is inside us) is the only real source of supply is peaceful and confident. He or she feels rich regardless of outside circumstances. Their thoughts will produce creative ideas, and they will prepare for the opportunities that are all around them because of the feeling of abundance that came first.

Eckhart Tolle in his book "A New Earth: Awakening to Your Life's Purpose" says:

"The ego identifies with having, but its satisfaction in having is a relatively shallow and short-lived one. Concealed within it remains a deep-seated sense of incompleteness, of not enough...the ego really means I am not enough yet."

Tolle goes on to examine the concept of ownership. He points out that if everyone agrees that you own "stuff", then you are wealthy. If people disagree, they will take your "stuff" away from you. He suggests that people constantly need something to identify with. Society has come up with laws and regulations to ensure that we all agree with the rules of "ownership."

Not only do we feel a need to accumulate more, we also want to make the ownership of "stuff" permanent. This is directly connected with our longing for immortality. Part of our strategy to achieve immortality includes having enough resources to last forever. However, the flaw in this strategy is that there never is "enough" to last forever. So we are in constant "accumulation mode." The key is to become aware of this primal fear which may stem from the days when our hunter/gatherer ancestors worried about not having enough food, shelter, and supplies.

Once we understand this motivator, we can deal with it. If we attempt to meet our basic need for long-term security by hoarding "stuff", we will never have enough and we will never feel satisfied.

You can't go back

Some people want to hold onto the past, which, they believe, is something that can never exist for them again, even if it is something that had held no satisfaction for them at the time. They have not yet learned the great truth that because you cannot go back, you have to go forward. There is nothing to go back to.

"Stuff" can take over your life

It is so easy for our lives to become dominated by things -- the work to get them, the effort to care for them, the need to buy insurance to protect them. On and on it goes.

Every time you consider purchasing something new you have to ask yourself if it will really improve your life, or will it just create more of a burden.

For years we spent our summers camping, but recently

we bought a summer cottage which needed extensive renovations (actually it probably should have been condemned). Suddenly our summers were no longer opportunities to read, relax and socialize with friends. First we needed to earn more money to buy the property, then we needed to come up with even more money to renovate it, and now it sucks up our time and money maintaining it.

Hoarding is a mental illness that will keep you poor

One of the first things we notice as we drive around wealthy neighborhoods is how clean everything is. Nothing is left lying around, everything is neatly put away. Every spring the yard waste and unwanted items are piled neatly at the curb.

Notice the contrast when you drive around poor neighborhoods. Broken toys, broken cars and garbage clutter the yards. The clutter is a symptom of the mindset that is keeping them poor. It doesn't cost anything to clean up.

The storage industry is big business in North America, catering to our obsession with hoarding "stuff". Billions of dollars are spent every month keeping items stuck in storage that are not being used, but are being kept "just in case" we ever need them.

We know of a vacant house where "stuff" had been stored for 10 years. This house was recently sold. The seller decided to move everything into storage, but when the movers went in to clean it out, most of the items had decomposed due to dampness over the years. The "stuff" they thought was worth keeping and paying to store had become worthless. It would have been better to let go of it years ago when it could have been of use to someone else.

We are no different, we have our own issues with "stuff." We have a storage locker in the basement of our condominium building. Because it is very full, we find it difficult to access anything in it. So we often end up buying the "stuff" again when we need it. The lesson was really brought home to us recently when a water pipe burst and flooded the area, including our "stuff." We realized that the things we had in there were not assets, but that they were liabilities. Our "stuff" was not worth storing and protecting if we did not use it.

Don't leave your kids to deal with your "stuff"

A member of our condominium board passed away. No one had any idea he was hoarding items until he died and his niece had to come and spend weeks cleaning out rooms and rooms of the "stuff" he had been accumulating. Most of his precious "stuff" ended up going to the dump.

Fighting over "stuff" can tear siblings apart when the parents die. In one previously very close family that we know, the oldest sister (who was the executor) packed her porch full of her father's "stuff". The overfilled porch is now useless and items stored there aren't being used by anyone. Other family members became very resentful about not getting what they perceived to be their share and relations have been strained ever since.

You really can't take it with you, so why not release what you don't need now and save your loved ones the trouble.

Prepare for prosperity

If you are not experiencing the abundance and prosperity you desire take a good hard look around you. Are there things that you are hanging onto unnecessarily? You can prepare for your prosperity by creating a vacuum to receive it. Nature can't stand an empty space and always rushes in to fill it. Get rid of what you no longer want or need. Do not keep clothing, furniture, books, or any other personal possessions that you no longer need or use. As long as you hoard this "stuff" it takes up space in your life and prevents good, new "stuff" from coming in.

So, bless your "stuff" and send it out into the universe to become someone else's riches.

6

Change how you think about security

*"The most secure individual is a life term convict in a penitentiary. Almost everything is cared for, thus he or she has little to worry about.
He or she has real security,
but at such a great price."*
**Eric Butterworth,
Spiritual Economics**

Security is elusive - by Mike

Security is an elusive thing; it is more psychological than financial. Most people cannot really define exactly what it would take to make them feel really secure.

When people think only of security, they stifle their personal growth and development. People even stay trapped in marriages that do not make them happy because they want to feel "secure".

Company benefits and seniority

So many people that I talk to feel trapped in jobs they hate, because they have good "benefits" and "seniority." But there is no security in a job. Your job can disappear overnight.

Employees at Enron thought the company was doing great until everything collapsed in just 4 days. People who had high wages, great benefits, and sizable pensions lost everything. Most of the employees had their life savings tied up in company stock, the value of which simply disappeared. They thought they had security because they worked for one of the largest corporations in the world.

I met a 26 year old man from a northern state who was struggling with a huge dilemma. He desperately wanted to move to Florida. The sunshine and the beach were really calling out to him, but he had a "good" job with the gas company, and had seniority and 6 years in toward his pension.

This was one of the saddest things I could imagine, a young man afraid to head out on an adventure because he was thinking about his retirement almost 40 years down the road. I tried to explain to him that there were no guarantees in life. No guarantee that the gas company would exist in 40 years, no guarantee that there would be any money to fund the pension plan at that time, and in fact, not even any guarantee that he would live long enough to retire.

Pension plans

New accounting rules have come into effect that require companies to report any expected shortfall in meeting funding required for retirement pensions. We are seeing many large companies reporting huge pension plan liabilities. What this means is that there will not be enough money available to pay the pensions employees are expecting to collect when they retire.

On top of that, government pension plans, such as social security, are "unfunded." This means that the money to pay pensions comes out of the employment contributions from people who are still working. This idea worked fine for our parents, the pre-war generation, but the retiring baby boom generation needs to have the generation that follows them, which is much smaller, finance their monthly pension payments. There may not be enough money to pay everyone. The government may have no choice but to reduce pension plan payments.

If you are relying on a pension to retire comfortably, you might have an unpleasant surprise.

Investments

Some people are relying on their investments to retire. They get a false sense of security from their investments, but, as we have seen over the past few years, investment gains can disappear overnight. Most of our public stocks have tumbled as the baby boom generation approaches retirement age and prepares to cash in their investments. They have been investing for years, anticipating living out their "golden years" in comparative comfort. Instead, stock price manipulation scandals and unscrupulous Ponzi schemers, such as Bernie Madoff, have crushed their dreams and sent them scrambling for part-time jobs in department stores and behind the counter at fast food outlets.

Other people have invested in real estate to provide for a good retirement. Real estate markets have also tumbled as a large segment of the population approaches retirement. People have had a false sense of security because most of their net worth has been measured by inflated real estate prices. The warm, fuzzy feeling quickly disappears when real estate values are slashed by 50% or more.

Possessions

People hoard material possessions in an attempt to feel secure, but security is not found in things.

Possessions are a trap because they give us a false sense of security. When people drive their cars, they feel secure inside their "metal shell." Road rage occurs because people feel "secure" enough within the safety of their cars to be very aggressive toward other drivers who are perceived to threaten their "safe" environment.

I remember how frightening it was for us to go off on an extended bicycle trip with only a few clothes and a tent. Leaving the protection of the "metal shell" is initially very intimidating. Our canoe trips also felt the same at first. However, once we realized that possessions, especially cars, do not really provide any protection, the feeling diminished.

Some people think their houses are the one place where they can feel safe. However, possessions, including houses, can be a trap. My father is afraid to leave his house because he has heart trouble and lives close to the ambulance depot. He is afraid that if he leaves home, the ambulance will not get to him in time. He feels trapped and will not attend family outings. He spends all his time at home.

Most self-made millionaires become rich, not because they want security, but because they are entrepreneurs, and risk takers, who love the excitement of the adventure. It is never really about the money, it is about the game. The money is just the way to keep score.

You are not secure because of the size of your bank account. You are not secure because of your investments or your possessions. Security comes from within. The only way that you will ever feel secure is by knowing that God is the source of your supply, by becoming a channel for the flow of infinite intelligence.

Ideas are the most valuable currency

God supplies us through ideas. Ideas are the most valuable currency of all. Once you understand this you can be secure in the knowledge that if you lost everything tomorrow you could get it all back and more with one good idea. Money can run out, things may wear out or get lost, but ideas endure.

Discard the notion that your welfare is tied to the economic fluctuations of the world. Things may happen around you, and things may happen to you, but the only things that really count are the things that happen inside you.

Gratitude

"A grateful mind is a great mind which eventually attracts to itself great things."
Plato

When we stop thinking in terms of God as a person we start to realize that God doesn't really care whether you are grateful or not. When you give thanks, when you are grateful it is for your benefit, not God's.

When you are grateful for what you have you are focusing on the good things in your life, and as we have pointed out throughout this book, what you focus on grows. As you focus on the good things, you attract to yourself more good things, and everything in your life begins to work in a more orderly and attractive way.

What I mean by gratitude is not the sort of ingratiating "thank you, thank you, I'm not worthy" groveling of a servant, but rather a sense of appreciation combined with a sense of deserving. As Florence Scovel-Shinn stated in all her books, we are children of God and as such we are entitled to receive good things.

Expressing gratitude in advance for what you want assumes that you will get it and creates a positive sense of expectancy that your wish is being fulfilled. It might not always be fulfilled in the manner you expect, but, nonetheless, it is done. Even when it does not work out the way you expected you will see that it turned out to be for your best. As long as you are in a grateful, creative mindset, the universe finds a way of helping you.

So, express a sense of gratitude for your car, your home, your employer, your investments and all your business transactions. Bless your money as you spend it, and bless your bills when they arrive. Doing so wields no magic power over these people, conditions, or things, but it does change you and the energy you radiate out into the world.

"Life is either a daring adventure or nothing.
Security does not exist in nature, nor do the
children of men as a whole experience it.
Avoiding danger is no safer
in the long run than exposure."

Helen Keller

Change how you think about giving

7

*"Give, and it shall be given unto you;
good measure, pressed down, shaken together,
running over, shall they give in to your bosom.
For with what measure ye mete it shall be
measured to you again."*
Luke 6:38

Giving is the key to getting

In order to receive, you must give. Look at all the possible opportunities for giving in your relationships with other people. Can you give more to your children or you neighbors? How about giving to strangers you meet? Consider the work you do as a gift to your employer or your customers. If you constantly think of ways you can give to others, you will be making room for you to receive.

Giving and sharing are very empowering. They reinforce your belief that your abundance is unlimited. In order to give, you have to be confident that you will get more. You have to know that what you give away will be replaced quickly and easily. You are not afraid that what you give away will be lost forever. In other words, instead of making decisions to give and to share based on fear, you make those decisions based on your confidence that your wealth is constantly increasing, not decreasing.

Giving does not diminish your supply because God is the source of your unlimited supply. When you truly believe this, you understand that giving and sharing cannot possibly limit your access to the resources of the universe.

In periods of economic slowdowns and downturns, the media are hard at work selling commercials by providing a constant stream of bad news. When listeners believe that things are spiraling downwards and that the future is bleak, they react negatively and think that the supply is limited. They stop spending and money stops changing hands. When money stops circulating, it stops being other people's supply and the prediction that things will get worse is self-fulfilling.

You always have something to give

The way to break the spiral is by giving and sharing, which starts up the prosperity cycle again. The items that you give away become the supply of those who are receiving.

Some people would argue that in tough economic times you might not have anything to give away. This is not true. You always have something that you can give away. It can be in many forms, including non-monetary. You can share your knowledge or time, as long as it is of value to other people.

When we let go of some of our money through giving, we find that we are freed of all the things that are attached to it, such as the fear of losing it or the anger if we perceive that someone is "after our money." When we give, we get rid of these bad feelings and they are replaced with good ones. Our experiences become more positive and we attract positive things.

If we give based on doing the best for others, good things will start to happen and positive events will enrich your life, opportunities and money just show up seemingly out of nothing and from nowhere. You should expect that to happen.

It is okay to expect that the universe will give back what you give out. You may even get back more than you gave. If you have found that your flow of money has dwindled, or stopped completely, giving is a good way of restarting the flow.

Often when people are broke they say something to the effect of "when some money comes in I will give a gift to the church or a charity." But when times are tough that is exactly when you should give first.

If you honestly have no money, go down to your church or some other nonprofit organization and volunteer your services. Go through your attic and closets and find all the seldom used "stuff" that is clogging up your life and give it away to someone who can really benefit from it. I'm not talking about all your garbage, I'm talking about good "stuff" that someone can really benefit from receiving. If you are unemployed give your services to some community group or offer to help someone who is struggling in a new business enterprise. Giving opens the floodgate for you to receive.

"You give before you get."
Napoleon Hill

Charity often perpetuates poverty

Don't think of your giving as charity. Think of it as expressing your appreciation for everything that you have been blessed with.

Charities perform a priceless service when they intervene and help in an emergency situation, such as giving protective shelter to battered wives. However, if your gift of money supports constant handouts to people who take them for granted and do not learn how to help themselves, then it is actually doing them more harm than good by not encouraging them to improve their own lot.

In addition to emergency help, we should provide resources that will help people become self-confident and self-sufficient. Would a gift of your time or of your special, unique skills perhaps be of more benefit?

Giving to help people help themselves is a gift that lasts a lifetime. Helping people change their self-image from a poor one to a rich one and providing life skills that last a lifetime is a greater contribution than just your money could provide.

"No one ever got rich by studying poverty and thinking about poverty. Do not talk about poverty; do not investigate it, or concern yourself with it. Never mind what its causes are; you have nothing to do with them. What concerns you is its cure. Do not spend your time in charitable work, or charity movements; all charity only tends to perpetuate the wretchedness it aims to eradicate. What tends to do away with poverty is not the getting of pictures of poverty into your mind, but getting pictures of wealth into the minds of the poor."

Wallace Wattles
The Science of Getting Rich

Self-sacrifice is no more noble than selfishness

Giving is good, but the universe does not expect self-sacrifice. The concept that martyrdom and suffering is supposed to earn you a place in heaven has been drummed into many people's minds. Hurting and depriving yourself is not good for your self-esteem. That programming should be replaced with one that lets you be you and takes advantage of your knowledge and experience. Believing your contribution is valuable is the first step in receiving money for your contribution.

"Remember that extreme altruism is no better and no nobler than extreme selfishness; both are mistakes. Get rid of the idea that God wants you to sacrifice yourself for others, and that you can secure his favor by doing so; God requires nothing of the kind."

Wallace Wattles
The Science of Getting Rich

Tithing your way to riches

"Bring ye the whole tithe into the storehouse ..... and prove me now here with, saith Jehovah of hosts, if I will not open you the windows of heaven, and pour you a blessing, that there shall not be room enough to receive it."
Malachi 3:10

Tithing in the old testament was basically paying taxes to the government. The payment was usually made by giving 10% of the crops that were harvested. As well, Israelites were expected to make additional free-will payments to support their church and their religious leaders.

Today many people consider "tithing" to mean giving 10% of your income to your church. I don't think we have to interpret it this narrowly. In my opinion, God's work does not mean just "church" work, it means promoting the best for everyone. If we give with the intention of helping others, or give out of a spirit of generosity and bounty the Universe will cooperate.

A portion of the money or "stuff" that you get should be given to people who can make good use of it. It does not mean that you have to give 10% to a religious organization, although you certainly can if you choose. What it does mean is a regular or "systematic" way of giving.

You can choose to give money or volunteer to the art community of your choice, directly to charitable organizations, or any other group or person you feel can benefit from your action.

"By the act of tithing, men make God their partner in their financial transactions and thus keep the channel open from the source in the ideal to the manifestation in the realm of things. Whoever thinks that he is helping to keep God's work going in the earth cannot help but believe that God will help him. This virtually makes God not only a silent partner but also active in producing capital from unseen and unknown sources..."
Charles Fillmore,
Prosperity

Do I have to give 10%? There is no real magic number to define how much you should give, perhaps 20 or 30% is more appropriate for you.

Giving with the right motivation works because it makes you feel good. Your mind is so much more positive when you are giving and this prepares the way for good things to happen to you.

As Forrest Gump says, ***"There is only so much money a man really needs, the rest is just for showing off."***

No one needs to have less so that I can have more

"What I want for myself,
I want for everybody."
Wallace Wattles,
The Science of Getting Rich

Some people barricade themselves in gated communities in order to feel "safe" from the outside world. Unfortunately, gated communities can become a prison. The need to create a place inside where we can control how things are is founded on the belief that the outside world is a dangerous place, full of poverty and crime.

However, if we assume that most people are basically good and honest, we would then see that everyone wants the same things: opportunities for their children, a comfortable place to live, a fulfilling and good-paying job, a nice home, etc. For example, eBay was founded on the belief that people are generally honest, and most of the time this is proven to be true.

Even the credit industry is based on the premise that the vast majority of people can be trusted to pay their bills.

So, expect the good and act accordingly.

Expect the good

When you have given or shared, you should expect to receive. Keep your mind open to receiving at least what you gave or shared. If you keep yourself centered in the universal consciousness, your good will come without strain or struggle.

If you are not getting what you want in life, ask your self, **"What is it that I can give so that I can receive?"**

"You can succeed best and quickest by helping others to succeed."

Napoleon Hill

8

Change how you think about work

*"Make yourself necessary to the world
and mankind will give you bread."*
Ralph Waldo Emerson

Bags of gold won't miraculously appear at your feet

The Quakers have an expression. ***"When you pray, move your feet."*** What they are saying is that we should not expect God to provide for us if we do not do our part.

In spiritual circles people talk a lot about "manifesting". Manifesting a mate, manifesting a new house, a new car, whatever. Some people make it sound like all of these things will just drop out of the sky and appear at your feet if you get the formula (the prayer) right. But it isn't quite that simple.

If we expect to get more, we have to be prepared to give more.

You can't get something for nothing

A friend called me in a panic. She suspected that she had been conned by an e-mail scam that promised her a large sum of money if she provided her personal information such as her bank account, passport number, driving permit number, etc. Although she was an intelligent woman with a successful career she had fallen for the idea that she could get something for nothing. Not surprisingly, the money had not arrived as promised and she was worried about her credit and other personal information being compromised. It cost her time and money to get the whole mess straightened out.

Con artists know that people fall for these scams all the time because we are all want the easy way, but the universe does not give you anything for nothing. You must give in order to receive.

Think of your work as giving

You cannot change your life from poverty to affluence unless you change your underlying thoughts and feelings toward work. We spend most of our lives engaged in some kind of gainful employment; so if your attitudes about working are not right, then you are sabotaging yourself.

Analyze your day. Are you eager to get to work in the morning? Is your work day an energizing happy experience? Or do you drag yourself out of bed in the morning and struggle through the day with one eye on the clock. If so, you are probably exhausted by the time you get home in the evening. You may claim to be exhausted from overwork, but if your only motivation is your paycheck you probably do as little as you can get away with. The exhaustion is more likely the result of the way you think about your work.

By changing how you think about your work, you can reignite your energy.

The world does not need any more assembly line workers

The days of graduating from high school, getting a unionized factory job, and retiring comfortably after 40 years are over.

Manufacturing companies, have found that they can no longer be competitive if they continue to pay workers current salaries. North American workers are losing their jobs in record numbers. So what are they supposed to do?

Become a creative entrepreneur

Even people who work for someone else have to start thinking like entrepreneurs. They have to continually ask "How can I help my company to be profitable?" Even if you are employed by someone, you are actually "self-employed." Employees must view their employment as selling their service to a customer, in their case, one particular customer, their employer. Employees have to view their employer's business as their own.

When walking in to a place of business, it is usually possible to tell whether someone is the business owner or an employee based on how hard they are willing to work to look after the customer. If you go into a store at closing time, you can really notice the difference in service. Employees often just want to get you out of the door while owners are willing to take the time to serve you if they think it will result in a sale.

If you can find creative ways to treat your employer's customer as if he or she were your own customer, you will be more valuable to your employer. In addition, you will be helping your employer's business survive and thrive.

Poor me, excuses for not producing

Most people make excuses for why they can't do something while other people with much bigger problems manage to achieve great things.

For example, my cousin Luc Polnicky became a quadriplegic after a tragic accident in a swimming pool in his early 20's. In spite of being unable to even get himself out of bed without help, he earned a Ph.D. and became the head of a rehab unit in a hospital which treats quadriplegic accident victims.

Another example is Irene's cousin Dan McGarvie, who after becoming paralyzed as a result of a hockey injury, is employed as a consultant to the insurance industry regarding how to best accommodate people with disabilities.

Another inspirational example is the world famous theoretical physicist, Stephen Hawking, who has made tremendous contributions to scientific research. He was diagnosed with ALS back in his 20's and wasn't expected to live very long. He is well known for his work on Einstein's theory of relativity. He has a Ph.D. in Physics and has written several books. He actually went into space on the space shuttle in April 2007. He is a Member of the US National Academy of Sciences. He has achieved all this with only the use of his brain.

Kind of makes you feel like a slacker doesn't it!

Their secret is that they have accepted their situation and have taken personal responsibility for their economic situation and have decided to make the most of their lives. Instead of blaming their disabilities, the economy, the politicians, and waiting for someone else to do something, they have taken matters into their own hands and have done something for themselves. They have decided that, regardless of the misfortunes that they have experienced, they alone are responsible for their personal happiness.

On the other hand, I know another woman who hated her job but instead of finding something else she liked better she managed to convince a doctor that she was too sick to work and got on welfare and disability. She spends her days playing video games and watching TV and blames everyone and everything else for her "bad luck."

How you interpret a situation makes all the difference

Two people can be in the same situation and interpret it entirely differently. For example, two people can get their layoff notices on the same day, one person looks at losing their job as a financial disaster. The other person looks at the same situation as an opportunity to move into a better paying, more enjoyable job, and that is what it turns out to be for them.

"Whether you think you can, or whether you think you can't, you're right."
Henry Ford

Work doesn't have to feel like a struggle

It's important to find work that feels like play. You will never get rich working, you just won't put in the time or the effort.

I know someone who is an entomologist. He absolutely loves bugs! He loves studying them so much that he would study bugs all the time even if he wasn't being paid for it. It doesn't feel like work for him. When he retires he will still be studying bugs. As a result he is very successful in his career.

For many years I worked in credit and collections. People would ask me all the time how I could work for so long in what many people feel is a distasteful career. I loved it. Collecting accounts is a game that I still love, so I am exceptionally good at it, and get paid extremely well for it as a result.

The key to success in any career is to see it as a game.

Take pride in your work, be the best you can be

Whatever it is that you are doing, give it your best shot. Be the best you can be. No one ever gets rich by being mediocre. If you are a gardener, be the best gardener you can possibly be. If you are a bookkeeper, give it your best. If you continuously work on being the best you can be you will always have work, and, if your present employer doesn't appreciate you, new opportunities will open up in front of you.

"The man who does more than he is paid for will soon be paid for more than he does."
Napoleon Hill

Everyone has something important to contribute

We are all interconnected and everyone's contribution is important. No one's job is any more important than another's. We see this very clearly whenever there is a garbage strike. When the garbage starts piling up you see how important a garbageman's job is.

If you are dissatisfied with your job, nothing will change until you decide to find your special niche, your unique contribution to the world, the special thing that you would do all day that does not feel like work.

Finding your perfect work

If you are dissatisfied with your present work situation as yourself the following questions:

What makes you happy?

Do you feel that your world is falling apart? Does nothing seem to be going right? Perhaps it's time to stop focusing on what is wrong and start focusing on what makes you really happy. And please don't tell me nothing makes you happy. Everyone has at least one and most people have a number of things that bring them joy. Start by listing the activities that make you happy. Don't try to put them in any order. Just write them down.

_____

_____

_____

_____

_____

_____

_____

_____

_____

What do you do really well?

From the list of activities that make you happy, pick out the ones that you do really well. Are they activities that come easily to you? Do they seem natural and require no effort on your part?

_____

_____

_____

_____

_____

_____

_____

_____

_____

_____

_____

_____

If money wasn't a concern and you knew you could not fail what would you do?

Does your short list of activities that make you happy and that you can do very well seem out of reach? Would it take too long to accomplish them? Do you lack the money? Do you tell yourself that they are just impossible dreams? Just imagine for a moment that those barriers are not there. Which one would you start with?

_____

_____

_____

_____

_____

_____

_____

_____

What difference do you want to make?

When you reach the end of your life, what difference do you want to have made? Which of your accomplishments do you want people to remember? Set some big goals and tell yourself that the only obstacles are those that you create. If you created them, you can eliminate them, since you are the one who is responsible. You are in charge.

_____

_____

_____

_____

_____

_____

_____

_____

_____

_____

Don't be afraid to experiment

What are your big goals? Set them, define them, visualize them, feel them, and you will attain them. Don't be afraid to strive to reach several goals simultaneously. Your goals can change, be traded for new ones, or be abandoned without guilt for bigger, better ones. It's up to you. You're in charge, you are responsible, you can do whatever you want that makes you happy.

Find the special talent within you, and use your unique talent to produce something the world can use.

_____

_____

_____

_____

_____

_____

_____

_____

_____

How will other people benefit from your product or service?

If you can answer this question and be able to explain it easily and quickly so that anyone can understand, you will have the ability to market your product or service.

_____

_____

_____

_____

_____

_____

_____

_____

_____

Do you really want to be of service?

We can never get something for nothing, but the world will supply all your needs in exchange for a product or service.

If you wait until you have all the money you think you will ever need before you begin to be of service with your special, unique talents, then you will never start. You will always feel that you never have quite enough. Instead, do it the other way around. If you focus on the special talent you have that lets you be of service to others, the money will be there for you. How you think is the secret to happiness and success.

"You can have everything in life you want, if you will just help other people get what they want."

Zig Ziglar

8 Steps to real financial security

9

Following these 8 steps will change your life:

Step 1 - Accept responsibility for your life, and release the past

The first step toward real financial security is to accept responsibility for your life. This means acknowledging that whatever your current financial situation is, you have created it through your thoughts, words, and actions. Quit blaming others for your financial woes.

Forgive people, and release grudges. We only hurt ourselves when we indulge in thoughts of resentment and blame.

Step 2 - Accept change

Change is inevitable; accept it. The world is not going back to the way things used to be. It is your choice; you can be like a surfer and ride the wave of the future or get swept away and drown in the undertow.

Step 3 - See the possibilities

Recognize that anything is possible. Make the effort to peek over the wall of mirrors that has kept you trapped. If anyone else has ever been able to change their life you can too. Read the biographies of successful people and emulate their best qualities. Travel, see the world, see the possibilities all around you. Nothing can hold you back but your own ignorance.

Step 4 - Get definite about what you really want

Decide what you really want. Most people have only a vague idea of what they want and so the results they get are vague and unsatisfying. Be specific about what prosperity really means to you.

We all want different things, so make sure that you are following your own dream, not someone else's vision. When you know what you want the universe will place ideas and opportunities in your path to get you there.

Spend some quiet time every day thinking about what you want, not from a perspective of lack as in "I wish I had", but visualize it as though you already have it. Write down exactly what you expect, keeping in mind that you can change your mind as your vision evolves.

Imagine the results as though you already have it. Picture what your life will look like, and imagine what it will feel like.

Step 5 - Indulge in "delusional" thinking

We know that what we focus on grows, so make a point of only paying attention to the things you want. Focus on what you want, ignore what you don't want.

Refuse to indulge in casual conversation about the bad economy, or about anything you do not want to grow in your life. Eliminate expressions such as "I can't," "I'm afraid," and "There is not enough" from your mind and your vocabulary. Talk only about the things you want to see happen. Picture the best for yourself and for others. Keep your thoughts centered on abundance, health and well-being for everyone.

Continually affirm something like: "My God is a God of plenty and I now receive all that I desire or require, and more."

Do something nice for someone every day. Smile. Recognize the spark of God inside of everyone.

Step 6 - Create a vacuum to receive

Give if you expect to receive. The universe will never give you something for nothing, so always be prepared to give. Think of your work and all your personal relationships as opportunities to give.

Clean out your closets, basement, and attic. Give away your good "stuff" to people who can use it, and recycle your garbage. Create a vacuum that will suck new good "stuff" into your life.

Step 7 - Act as if

Assume that your good is on its way to you even if it isn't here yet. Prepare for the thing you are expecting. Get excited! If you are anticipating a move, start packing. If you want a new car polish and clean up your current one so you it will be ready to trade in.

Step 8 - Think very carefully before you acquire any new "stuff"

More "stuff" doesn't necessarily mean a happier, more comfortable life. Think very carefully before you decide that you must have another car, a bigger house, the latest toy. This doesn't mean that you can't indulge yourself, that you can't have nice things, but often the things we think we want just add to our stress, not to our comfort.

"You are today where your thoughts have brought you. You will be tomorrow where your thoughts take you."
James Allen

Recommended Reading

10

If you are interested in reading more about money and Spirituality we highly recommend the following books:

Books by Florence Scovel-Shinn

"The Game of Life and How to Play It"
"The Secret Door to Success"
"The Power of the Spoken Word"
"Your Word is Your Wand"

Florence Scovel-Shinn's books should be daily reading for anyone who wants to change the way they think and speak about their finances.

"Spiritual Economics" by Eric Butterworth

Eric Butterworth was a Unity Minister in New York City. This book is wonderful for helping you change the way you think about finances, health, relationships, all facets of prosperity.

"The Science of Getting Rich" by Wallace D. Wattles
This is the book that inspired "The Secret". A classic.

Books by Catherine Ponder

"Open Your Mind to Prosperity"
"Dare to Prosper"
"The Secret of Unlimited Prosperity"
"The Dynamic Laws of Prosperity"
"The Millionaires of the Bible series"
Catherine Ponder is a Unity Minister and inspirational author who has written more than a dozen books about prosperity.

"Prosperity" by Charles Fillmore
Charles Fillmore was the founder of the Unity Movement, this book is a classic.

"Your Faith is Your Fortune" by Neville Goddard
According to Neville, we are the creator of our lives. This is a very inspirational, thought provoking book.

"Think and Grow Rich" by Napoleon Hill
Originally published in 1937, this book has sold more than 60 million copies

"The Secret of the Ages" by Robert Collier
Originally published in 1926, this book has inspired many of the prosperity books since.

About the authors

What makes us think that we are qualified to write a book about money and spirituality?

Mike: I can talk from experience when it comes to the expectations of "security" that a good education and a management job is supposed to provide. I grew up in a middle-class family. All my relatives are professionals and the expectation was that I would get a good education and then a secure job with a pension.

I have had every advantage possible, a loving family, almost "enough" money, a private school education, and parents who were willing and able to pay for my university education. So of course, I screwed it up. I managed to fail my first year of university and got married at 19. There I was with no job, no education, and a family of my own to support. I was facing a very different future than the one my parents had envisioned for me. I spent the next 16 years struggling to get an education while working full time. This took a toll on my marriage and I ended up divorced. I was broke and found myself having to start over with nothing.

Twelve years later I was happily remarried and had more than enough letters after my name to play scrabble with. I am a Certified Public Accountant and hold the top credit designations in the US, Canada, and the UK, have a Bachelor's Degree in Administrative Studies, and a Master's Degree in Business Administration so depending on which order you place them it goes Mike Morley B. Admin., MBA, CPA, CCE, MICM, CCP.

I had a very well paying job with a large multinational corporation that was driving me crazy. My health was suffering from the corporate stress and the 80-hour work weeks, but I didn't think I had any other choices. Fortunately my wife convinced me that she would rather be broke and have me alive and happy than be able to collect on my life insurance.

At this point I realized that if something didn't change I would be following in the footsteps of my father who developed numerous health problems by age 57 and was never able to go back to work, and my Uncle Teddy, a physician, who barely made it to retirement before dying of a heart attack.

So I left the "security" of the corporate world to start out on my own. I literally had to take a leap of faith that things would work out. It was terrifying at first, but since then I have discovered that God really is the source of my supply. There have been, and continue to be, some amazing events that have proven this to me. That was nearly 10 years ago.

Sure, as every self-employed business person knows, there have been lots of times since where I didn't have a clue where the next dollar was coming from, but the universe always comes through. Am I rich? Well, it depends on your definition. If you mean am I a millionaire, the answer is no, not yet, but I have a lifestyle that most people would envy. I spend part of my winter in the sun and my summers at my cottage. I only accept jobs that excite me, and are intellectually stimulating and I get plenty of them. Sure, I don't have a pension, but neither will many of the people who currently think they do (the under-funding of pension plans will be the next big financial shock to hit the financial news) and since I work at things I enjoy I plan to work till the day I cross over to the other side, so I don't worry about retirement.

For me, the continuing challenge is being aware of what I am thinking. Even today, once in a while, I catch myself slipping into old habits and must continue to be vigilant about correcting myself because I know that it will affect my financial decisions and my life.

Irene: Except for short periods of employment I have always been self-employed, so for me depending on the universe to meet my needs has never been as much of a challenge as it has been for Mike. I realized early in life that I didn't like being an employee so I really never experienced the kind of trap that a well-paying corporate job can be.

This book is not about choosing to be self-employed, it is not our intention to place restrictions on how the universe provides for anyone; it is about recognizing that regardless of how we earn our living, our security is inside of us. We do not need to be dependent on other people or external circumstances for our well-being.

Other Books by Irene McGarvie

The Sweat Lodge is For Everyone

ISBN 978-0-9737470-6-5 $19.95

The Native American Sweat Lodge Ceremony offers so many benefits, both spiritual and physical for anyone who has the opportunity to take part in one.

This book is the non-Native's guide to understanding, participating in, and benefiting from Native American Sweat Lodge ceremonies.

Messages in Your Tea Cup

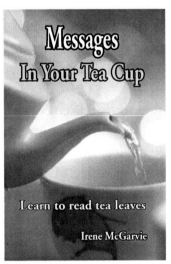

ISBN 978-0-9783939-6-0 $19.95

Have you ever wished that you could predict the future? Throughout history people all over the world have been able to predict future events and get advice from"beyond" through tea leaf reading.

This book will teach you everything that you need to know to begin reading tea leaves immediately.

Index

www.learnancientwisdom.com

CPSIA information can be obtained at www.ICGtesting.com
Printed in the USA
270513BV00004B/20/P